DOMINOES

Eight G
American Tales

LEVEL TWO 700 HEADWORDS

OXFORD
UNIVERSITY PRESS

Great Clarendon Street, Oxford OX2 6DP

Oxford University Press is a department of the University of Oxford.
It furthers the University's objective of excellence in research, scholarship, and education by publishing worldwide in

Oxford New York

Auckland Cape Town Dar es Salaam Hong Kong Karachi
Kuala Lumpur Madrid Melbourne Mexico City Nairobi
New Delhi Shanghai Taipei Toronto

With offices in

Argentina Austria Brazil Chile Czech Republic France Greece
Guatemala Hungary Italy Japan Poland Portugal Singapore
South Korea Switzerland Thailand Turkey Ukraine Vietnam

First published in Dominoes 2008

2024

23

ISBN: 978 0 19 424890 7 Book
ISBN: 978 0 19 463954 5 Book and Audio Pack

Printed in China

This book is printed on paper from certified and well-managed sources.

ACKNOWLEDGEMENTS

Illustrations by: Jamel Akib

The publisher would like to thank the following for permission to reproduce photographs: Getty Images pp31 (Museum of the City of New York/Byron Collection/Hulton Archive), 56 (Ford Model T/ Car Culture), 58 (market/Ewing Galloway/Hulton Archive), 60 (winter sale/Derek Berwin), 60 (Central Park zoo 1886/Wallace G. Levison/Time Life Pictures); iStockphoto p18 (palette/ Clayton Hansen); Mary Evans Picture Library p60 (boarding house/Living London); OUP pp25 (old fashioned iron/Design Pics), 39 (wedding cake/Photodisc), 56 (earthquake damaged buildings/Photodisc); Shutterstock p56 (Orville Wright/Everett Historical).

DOMINOES

Series Editors: Bill Bowler and Sue Parminter

Eight Great American Tales

O. Henry

Text adaptation by Bill Bowler

Illustrated by Jamel Akib

O. Henry was the pen name of William Sidney Porter (1862–1910). Born in Carolina, Porter left school early to work in drugstores, on cattle farms, and as a journalist. In prison for three years for taking money from a bank where he worked, Porter began writing short stories for newspapers and magazines. The eight tales in this book – *Fine furs for a lady, Springtime on the menu, The last leaf, The things we do for love, Ikey Schoenstein's love-potion, The Count and the wedding guest, Thinking yourself rich,* and *Lost and found* – are among his finest.

OXFORD
UNIVERSITY PRESS

ACTIVITIES

BEFORE READING

1 Match the words with the pictures.

a ☐ a criminal
b ☐ a travelling salesman
c ☐ a sheriff
d ☐ a policeman
e ☐ a farmer
f ☐ an artist
g ☐ a shopkeeper
h ☐ a waiter

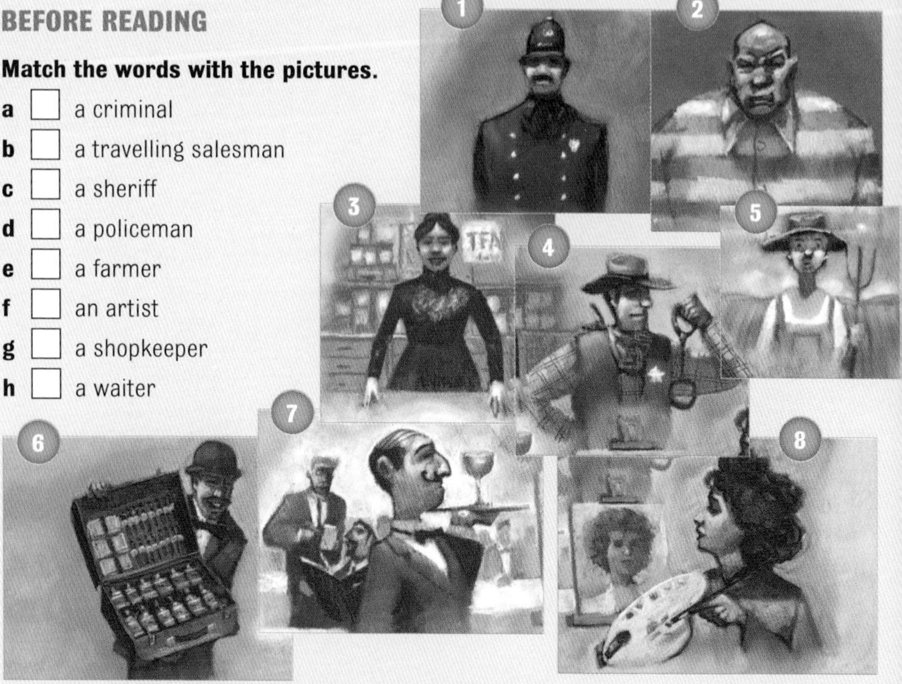

2 The stories in this book all happen in the United States of America between 1899 and 1910. Which of the people in Activity 1 do you think that you will read about?

3 Which of these sentences about life in the United States in the early 1900s are true? Discuss your ideas with a partner.

a New York City suddenly got bigger. ☐
b The Ford factory started to make cars. ☐
c The Wright brothers flew in an aeroplane for the first time. ☐
d Everyone listened to radio from all over the world. ☐
e People started to travel by subway trains under (and over) New York City. ☐
f Most women made all the clothes for their families. ☐
g Many people went to Broadway to see theatre with songs, and dancing. ☐
h American football was America's favourite sport. ☐
i Only men – not women – chose the politicians who went to Washington. ☐

Story 1

Fine furs for a lady

When '**Kid**' Brady fell in love with Molly McKeever, he decided to leave the criminal **gang** that he belonged to.

His gang worked in the west of New York, between Eleventh and Twelfth **Avenues**, near the river. By day, they stood lazily on street corners in their fine suits, occasionally speaking quietly to each other. But their real business was taking money from the good people of New York. Mostly they preferred to do this without any noise, or any blood. But any New Yorkers who weren't happy to lose their money in this way soon found themselves either in the hospital or the name of a newly dead person in a police notebook.

When Brady told the others that he was leaving the gang, they were sorry. He was the finest, strongest, and cleverest of them all. But they didn't try to stop him. For criminals like them, it was neither wrong nor unmanly to do what your girlfriend wanted.

kid an informal name for a young man, often with a good-looking baby face

gang a number of people who work on a crime

avenue a big street, often with trees at the sides

'OK,' Brady told Molly one night when she was asking him to end his life of crime. 'I'll get a job, and in a year I'll marry you. We can get somewhere nice to live.'

'Oh, Kid,' said Molly, 'That's great. We can be happy with just a little.'

'But,' said Brady, 'I won't have money for good suits like before. That'll be hard.'

'Don't worry. I'll love you just the same.'

So Brady started working as a **plumber**. That was what he studied when he was younger. For eight months he worked hard, and stayed true to Molly.

Then, one day, he came home with a strange **parcel**.

'Open that, Moll,' he said quietly. 'It's for you.'

Molly took off the paper, screamed happily, and put something long, dark, and soft around her neck.

'The best Russian **furs**,' said Brady.

'Thank you, Kid,' said Molly. 'I never had any furs before. But aren't Russian furs expensive?'

'Could I ever buy you anything cheap? Hey, Moll, you look great in them.'

plumber someone who mends baths and toilets

parcel a paper box with things in

fur the hair on an animal's body

Then he saw Molly looking at him with **sad** eyes. He knew what that look meant.

'I paid for them with good money,' he said.

'Sure. With the $75 dollars a month that you get from working as a plumber.'

'Look, I had some money from before, too. I left the gang for you, Moll, remember? Now put on those furs, and let's go out for a walk.'

So they went for a walk. Fine Russian furs were big news for the poor people living on that side of New York. Soon everyone was talking about them.

Detective Ransom was walking down the street not far behind them.

'Why is everyone so excited?' he asked one man standing on a street corner.

'Kid Brady got his girlfriend the best Russian furs, they say. Has anyone lost any expensive furs lately?'

'But Brady left the gang, didn't he? Now I heard that he's working at his old job.'

'Right. But some say that he paid $900 for those furs. How can a plumber find money like that?'

Ransom walked faster, and soon found Brady and Molly walking slowly along the street.

'Can I speak to you for a minute?' he asked quietly, touching Brady's arm.

Brady looked at him angrily.

'Were you at Mrs Hethcote's house on West Seventh Street yesterday, mending a water **pipe**?'

'Yes,' said Brady. 'Why?'

'The old **lady**'s thousand dollar Russian furs left the house at about the same time that you did. The way that Mrs Hethcote described them, they're just like the ones that the young lady's wearing.'

sad not happy

pipe a long narrow thing that water goes through in a house

lady a woman from a good family

'Ransom,' Brady began, 'I bought those furs today at–' and then he stopped.

'OK. So let's go to the shop where you bought the furs – with the lady – and find out if what you're saying is true.'

'Let's do that,' said Brady hotly.

Then he looked suddenly across at Molly's worried face and smiled strangely.

'It's no good,' he said suddenly, 'You're right, Ransom. They're the Hethcote furs. Molly, you'll have to give them to the police.'

Molly, her eyes full of **tears**, held Brady's arm.

'Oh, Kid, how could you do it? I was so pleased with you, and now they'll send you to **jail** – and where's our happy life together?'

'Come on, Ransom,' said Brady wildly, 'Take the furs. I'm ready. Wait a minute, I think I'll . . . No . . . I can't. Molly, go home.'

Just then, Policeman Kohen came round the corner. Ransom stopped him and explained about the furs.

'Sure. I heard about the Hethcote furs,' said Kohen, 'And you say that these are the same. Can I see them? I sold furs when I was younger.'

He looked at the furs carefully.

'These are Alaskan, not Russian. And they cost about twenty doll . . . '

Suddenly Brady hit Kohen in the face, Molly screamed, and Ransom quickly put some **handcuffs** on the 'Kid'.

'They cost about twenty dollars only,' Kohen went on, 'not a thousand.'

Brady's face turned red.

'You're right,' he said, 'I paid $21.50 for them. But I was ready to go to prison for six months for Molly never to know how much they really cost. I hate cheap things.'

Molly put her arms round his neck.

tear the water that comes from your eye when you cry

jail prison

handcuffs policemen put these circles of metal with locks on them around prisoners' hands to stop them from escaping easily

'Look, I don't want expensive furs, or lots of money. I just want you, Kid,' she said.

'Take the handcuffs off him, Inspector,' said Kohen. 'While I was leaving the police station, I heard the latest news about the Hethcote furs. The old lady found them at the back of her **wardobe**. Young man, I'll forget about you hitting me – just this once.'

Just before the policemen left, Ransom gave Molly back her furs. She smiled at Brady and put them round her neck again like a real lady.

wardrobe a big piece of furniture where you put things to wear

ACTIVITIES

READING CHECK

Match the sentences with the people. You can use some names more than once.

- **a** [1] is in a criminal gang before he meets Molly McKeever.
- **b** [ ] wants Kid to have a real job.
- **c** [ ] doesn't think that Brady bought the furs.
- **d** [ ] tells the police that someone stole her expensive Russian furs.
- **e** [ ] wants to go with Kid and Molly to the fur shop.
- **f** [ ] doesn't want Molly to know how much the furs cost.
- **g** [ ] tells everyone that Molly's furs aren't from Russia.
- **h** [ ] doesn't mind that the furs aren't expensive.

1

2

3

4

5

WORD WORK

Complete the crossword using the pictures.

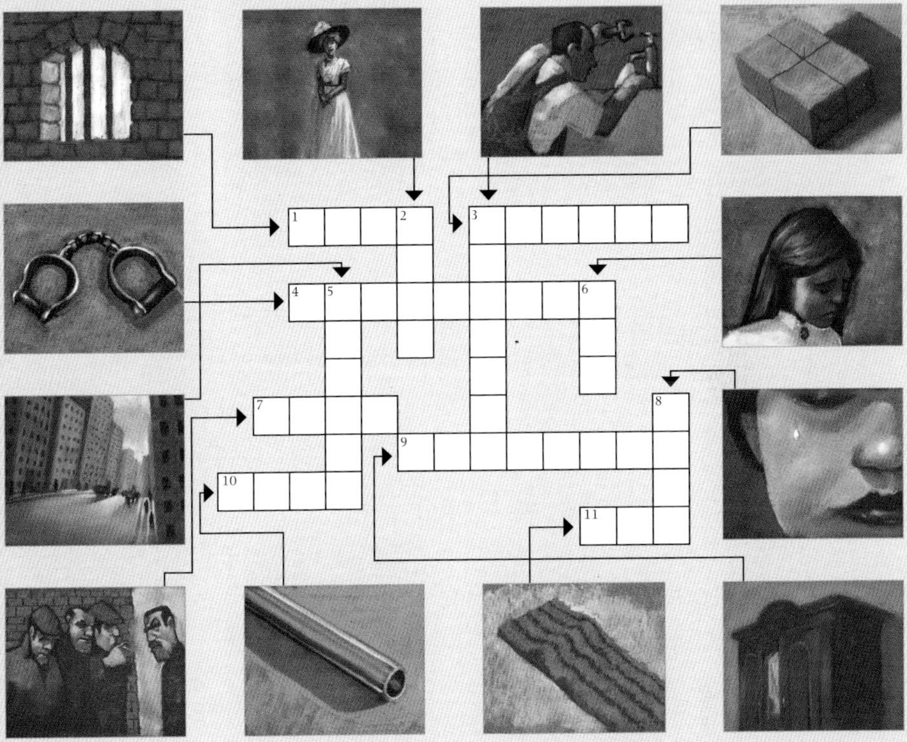

GUESS WHAT

Tick the words that best describe the main characters in the next story.

- ☐ angry
- ☐ beautiful
- ☐ excited
- ☐ hungry
- ☐ interesting
- ☐ lonely
- ☐ poor
- ☐ sad

Sarah

Walter

- bored ☐
- clever ☐
- dangerous ☐
- friendly ☐
- kind ☐
- nice ☐
- rich ☐
- worried ☐

Story 2

Springtime on the menu

It was a March day in Manhattan, and Sarah was crying over her menu.

Perhaps you think that she was sad because she was eating carefully and didn't want to see **ice cream** on the menu. Well, you're wrong.

Sarah was sitting at her desk with a **typewriter** in front of her. She worked at home – **typing** things for people.

Her best job was working for Schulenberg's Restaurant. This stood next to the house where she had a room. When she ate there one winter evening, she noticed that the writing on the menu **card** was really difficult to understand.

That night she typed out the menu, and the next day she showed it to Mr Schulenberg. He at once gave her the job of typing out menus for his restaurant every day. For this work Mr Schulenberg agreed to pay Sarah in food.

After that, a **waiter** took three meals every day to Sarah's room together with the new menu of the day in pencil for Sarah to type.

Now it was an afternoon in March – springtime! But the weather was still as cold as winter, and Sarah felt sad. She looked out of her window at the factory opposite, but she didn't really see it. She was remembering her holiday in the country last summer.

Sarah stayed two weeks at Sunnybrook **Farm**. There she fell in love with old Farmer Franklin's son, Walter. He took her for long walks in the country, and one day they sat together under a tree and he made a **crown** of **dandelion** flowers and put it on her head.

'Those yellow flowers look really beautiful in your brown hair,' said Walter.

ice cream sweet food that is made from very cold, thick milk

typewriter something that people wrote things quickly with before computers

type to write on a computer or typewriter

card a piece of thick paper

waiter someone working in a restaurant who takes food to people

farm a house with land in the country

crown a king or a queen wears this on their head

dandelion a wild plant with yellow flowers and leaves that you can cook and eat

And Sarah walked back to the farm house with the dandelion crown on her head, and her hat in her hand.

'I'm going to marry you first thing next spring,' said Walter and his eyes shone.

And then Sarah came back to the big city and her work as a typist.

Suddenly a knock on her room door made her forget those happy days. It was the waiter from Schulenberg's with the new menu.

She put a white card in the typewriter and began.

Her fingers danced across the typewriter keys. The **soups** were first. The meats came next. After that, it was the vegetables – potatoes, carrots, tomatoes, and then – Sarah was crying over the menu.

soup a food that you make by cooking vegetables or meat in water

She was waiting for a letter from Walter, and during the past two weeks no letter came. And now, on the menu that she was typing, she read 'dandelions' and something about an egg. She remembered Walter making that dandelion crown for her, and saying that he wanted to marry her in the spring, and now – seeing those beautiful flowers as just something to eat on the menu in front of her – she felt terrible.

At last she stopped crying. For a while she touched the keys of the typewriter sadly, still thinking of her young farmer friend. But soon she was busy typing card after card.

At six o'clock, the waiter from Schulenberg's brought her dinner, and took away the finished menus.

After dinner, Sarah took a book from the table, sat down in a comfortable chair, and began to read.

Just then, there was a ring at the front door. The **landlady** opened it. Sarah put down her book, and listened.

Hearing a man's voice downstairs, she suddenly jumped up from her chair, opened her room door, and ran out to the top of the stairs.

There, running up the stairs towards her, was Walter – and soon she was in his arms.

'Why didn't you write?' she asked.

'I wanted to surprise you. So I went to your old address, but they told me that you weren't living there. I didn't know where to find you.'

'But I wrote to you with my new address.'

'I never got it.'

'So how did you find me?'

The young farmer smiled.

'Well, I went to the restaurant next door for dinner, and looked at the menu. When I got to just below tomatoes, I jumped out of my chair, and called for Mr Schulenberg. He told me where you lived.'

landlady a woman who gets money for renting out rooms

'I remember,' said Sarah softly, 'Dandelions came just below tomatoes.'

'I knew that it was your typing, because of the strange way that your typewriter types the Ws higher than the other letters.'

'But there isn't a letter W in "dandelion"!' cried Sarah in surprise.

The young man took a menu from his pocket and gave it to her.

At the top there was a round grey **mark** from one of her tears. Sarah knew that it was the card she was typing when she began crying about the summer. And, there – just below tomatoes – in place of dandelions, she read:

mark something dirty of a different colour that you see on something

DEAREST WALTER, WITH AN EGG ON TOP

ACTIVITIES

READING CHECK

Are these sentences true or false? Tick the boxes.

		True	False
a	Sarah is working in Schulenberg's Restaurant when the story starts.	☐	☑
b	Mr Schulenberg pays her for typing out the menus.	☐	☐
c	Sarah is thinking about her summer holiday.	☐	☐
d	Walter and Sarah wanted to get married in the summer.	☐	☐
e	Sarah is crying because Walter hasn't written to her for two weeks.	☐	☐
f	Something on the menu makes Sarah remember Walter.	☐	☐
g	Walter didn't write to Sarah because he didn't have her address.	☐	☐
h	The people at Sarah's old house gave Walter her new address.	☐	☐
i	Walter found Sarah because of the typing on the menu.	☐	☐

WORD WORK

Find the words in the pictures to complete the sentences.

a Sarah wrote out the menus on pieces of c a r d .

b Elizabeth II wore her _ _ _ _ _ to the party.

c There are a lot of _ _ _ _ _ _ _ _ _ _ _ in the garden this year.

d Walter has always lived on a _ _ _ _ .

e I love chocolate _ _ _ _ _ _ _ _ .

f You usually pay the _ _ _ _ _ _ _ _ for the flat at the end of the month.

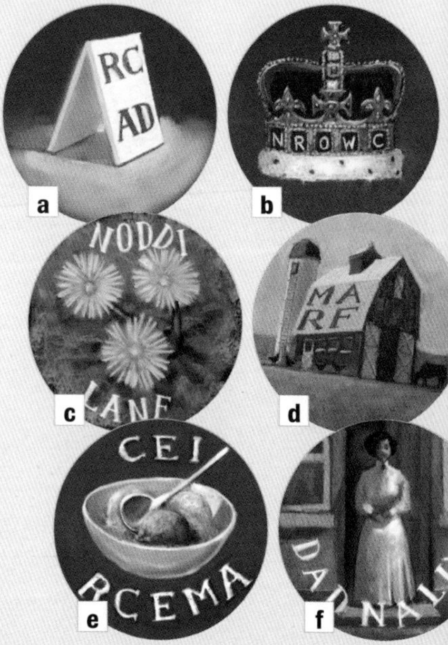

g I can't get this black _ _ _ _ off your shirt.

h We eat a lot of _ _ _ _ when it's really cold in the winter.

i The letter 'w' on Sarah's _ _ _ _ _ _ _ _ _ _ doesn't work very well.

j 'Can you see the _ _ _ _ _ _ ? I want to pay.'

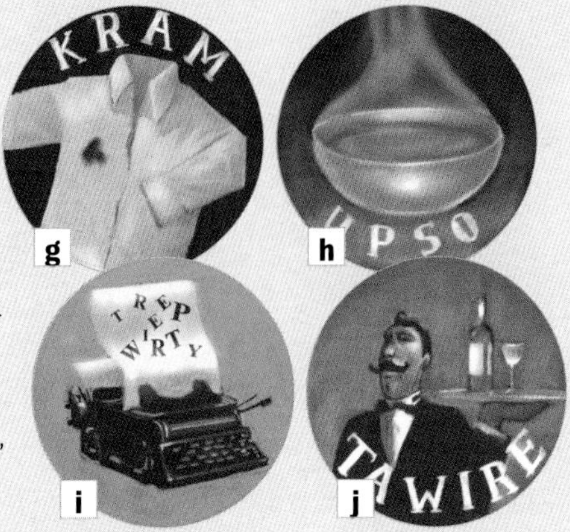

GUESS WHAT

The next story is about two women in New York. Look at the picture. What do you think you will read about in the story? Tick three things.

a They both come from rich country families. ☐
b They live together in the same flat. ☐
c They work together in an Italian restaurant. ☐
d One of them becomes very ill. ☐
e One of them loses her job. ☐
f An old man helps them. ☐

Story 3

The last leaf

Sue and Joanna had the top floor of a house in Greenwich Village, where everyone in the New York **art** world lives. Sue came from Maine, and Joanna from California. They met in May in an Italian restaurant on Eighth Street. They liked each other at once, their tastes were the same, and so they decided to live together. Both were artists.

Now it was November – cold, windy and wet – and **pneumonia** was in town.

Joanna was ill in bed with it. Sue and the doctor spoke outside her bedroom door.

'Will she live?' asked Sue.

'It's a one in ten **chance**. But she must *want* to live. What does she have to live for?'

'Well, she'd like to **paint** a picture of Naples one day.'

'Paint?! No. That's not good enough. I mean is she interested in a man, for example?'

'No, Doctor,' said Sue. 'There's no man in her life.'

'What bad luck!' said the doctor. 'I'll do all that I can. But I'm not hopeful.'

When the doctor left, Sue cried for a while. Then she went busily into Joanna's room with her **drawing** book, singing a happy song.

Joanna's eyes were closed. 'She's asleep,' thought Sue, and stopped singing.

She sat down by the window, and began drawing a picture of a young farm worker for a **magazine**. Suddenly she heard Joanna speaking softly. She went to her.

Joanna's eyes were open now, and she was counting aloud – counting down. 'Twelve,' she said, and after a while, 'Eleven . . . ten . . . nine,' and then, 'Eight, seven, six,' nearly at the same time.

art pictures and other things to look at; music, painting, writing, the theatre, and the cinema are all arts

pneumonia people sometimes become ill with this in cold, wet weather; when you get it badly it can kill you

chance the possibility that something can happen

paint to put different colours on paper to make a picture

draw (*past* **drew, drawn**) to make a picture with a pen or pencil

magazine a thin book with lots of pictures; you can buy it every week or every month

Sue looked out of the window. She saw only the wall of the next house, with an old yellow and green **ivy plant** that climbed up it. The half-dead plant had few leaves on it because of the autumn winds.

'There are only five, now,' said Joanna.

'Five what, dear? What are you counting?'

'The ivy leaves,' replied Joanna. 'When the last one goes, I'll die. I've known that for two days. Didn't the doctor tell you about it?'

'Joanna, don't say that. It doesn't matter what happens to that old plant. It has nothing to do with you. Now, eat some soup and I'll finish my picture.'

'I don't want any soup,' said Joanna, looking out of the window, 'Now there are only four.'

ivy a climbing plant that grows on walls and the sides of trees

plant a small green thing, with leaves and, sometimes with flowers

'Joanna dear, try to sleep. I must ask Mr Berman to come up. I want to draw a picture of him as a poor old farmer. I won't be long.'

Mr Berman, who was over sixty years old, lived downstairs. He was a painter too, but he never sold anything, and he drank a lot. He had a wonderful face, just right for Sue's magazine picture.

Sue told him all about Joanna feeling that she was going to die when the last ivy leaf fell.

'She can't really think that this will happen! The poor woman!' he cried.

'She's thinking very strangely these days,' said Sue.

When they went upstairs, Joanna was asleep. Sue closed her window **blind** and left the room.

In Sue's work room, she and Berman looked worriedly out of the window at the old ivy plant. Then Berman sat, and Sue drew him in half an hour.

The next day Sue woke up early. She heard a call from Joanna's room.

'Open the window blind,' Joanna said when she arrived.

Once the blind was open, they both saw one last leaf on the ivy plant.

'Oh,' said Joanna. 'With all that wind and rain last night I'm surprised. But I'm sure it'll fall today, and then I'll die.'

The day was a windy one, but – all through it – the last leaf stayed. And on the morning of the next day, too, the leaf was still there.

'Susie,' said Joanna then, 'I've been a bad girl. That last leaf is telling me that it was very wrong of me to want to die. Bring me some soup, dear.'

An hour later she said, 'One day I'll paint Naples.'

That afternoon the doctor told Sue, 'She has a one in two chance.'

The next day, he said, 'She's out of danger. But poor Mr Berman downstairs is dying of pneumonia. There's no hope for him, I'm afraid.'

That afternoon Sue went into Joanna's bedroom.

'Joanna dear, Mr Berman died today – of pneumonia. And do you know why? One terrible, cold, wet night he took a **ladder** and some green and yellow paints and he climbed up, and – Oh, look at that last ivy leaf on the wall! Why didn't it ever move in the wind? Can't you see? It was Mr Berman's last great picture. He painted it there the night that the last leaf fell.'

blind people close this in front of a window at night to stop people looking in

ladder you use this for climbing up or down tall buildings or other things

READING CHECK

Who are the sentences about? Tick the columns.

	Sue	*Joanna*	*Mr Berman*
a . . . is an artist.	☑	☑	☑
b . . . gets very ill.	☐	☐	☐
c . . . wants to paint a picture of Naples.	☐	☐	☐
d . . . is drawing some pictures to sell.	☐	☐	☐
e . . . thinks that she will die when an old plant dies.	☐	☐	☐
f . . . has a wonderful face to draw.	☐	☐	☐
g . . . tells Mr Berman about the last leaf on the plant.	☐	☐	☐
h . . . starts to get better when the last leaf doesn't fall.	☐	☐	☐
i . . . paints a picture of a leaf on a wall.	☐	☐	☐
j . . . dies near the end of the story.	☐	☐	☐

WORD WORK

1 Use the words in the wordsnake to answer the questions.

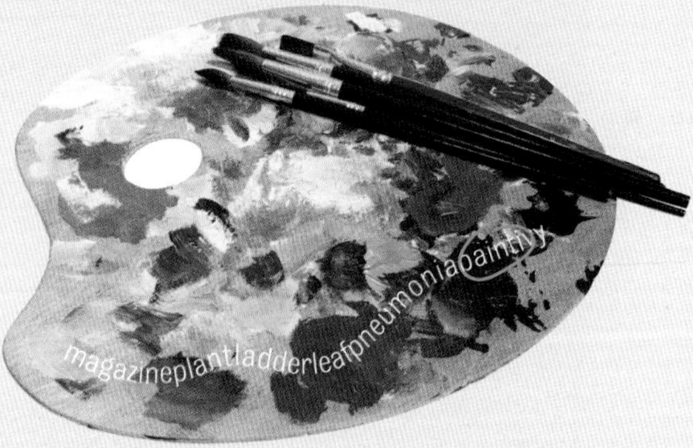

a What does Joanna want to do in Naples? paint.

b What has Joanna got? ______________ .

c What is Sue's picture of the farmers for? A ______________.

d What can Joanna see out of the window from her bed? A big old _______ _______ .

e What does Mr Berman paint on the wall? A _______.

f What does Mr Berman climb up to paint his last picture? A _______.

2 Correct the black words in these sentences.

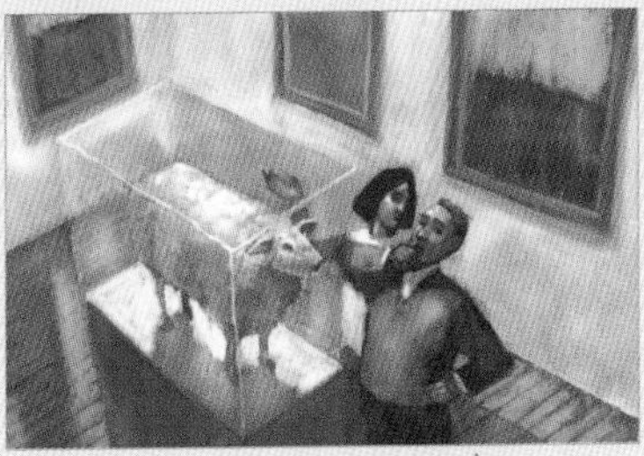

a 'How they can call that ~~**ark**~~ art!'

b Spain have a good **change** of winning.

c The **blings** are down. Nobody's home.

d Amy *can* **dream** well. This picture's great!

GUESS WHAT

The next story is *The things we do for love*. What do you think happens in it? Tick the best options.

a Two young artists . . .
- **1** ☐ fall in love and get married.
- **2** ☐ meet and become good friends.
- **3** ☐ move to New York and become famous.

b To make some money . . .
- **1** ☐ the man sells his paintings.
- **2** ☐ the woman gives music lessons.
- **3** ☐ they both find badly paid jobs.

c They lie to each other because . . .
- **1** ☐ they fall in love with different people.
- **2** ☐ they don't want to worry each other.
- **3** ☐ they don't want to show their love.

Story 4

The things we do for love

As a boy, Joe Larabee was famous in the town in Middle America where he lived because he could paint beautifully. At twenty, he went to study in New York.

Delia Carruthers was from the South, and played music wonderfully as a girl. When she was eighteen, her family paid for her to study in New York.

Joe and Delia met one day in the big city, fell in love, and soon after got married. They went to live in a little flat far from the centre.

Joe studied painting with Mr Magister, and Delia studied music with Mr Rosenstock. They were very happy while their money lasted.

But soon they couldn't pay for more classes with Magister and Rosenstock, who were expensive. So Delia said she would give music lessons to get some money.

After two days, she came home excitedly.

'I've found a student,' she said. 'Her name's Clementina. She's **General** A. B. Pinkney's daughter. They live in a wonderful, big house on Seventy-First Street. Clementina's only eighteen, wears white, and is a lovely girl. I'm going to give her three lessons a week, for five dollars each. Just think. When I get more students, I can go back to Rosenstock.'

'I can't let you do all the work,' said Joe. 'I must get a job too, even if it's only selling newspapers in the street.'

'Oh, no, Joe,' replied Delia, 'You mustn't stop your classes with Magister.'

'All right,' said Joe. 'I really don't like you giving lessons. It isn't art. But you're a dear to do it.'

'When you love your art, nothing is too hard,' said Delia softly.

general a very important person in an army

'Well, Tinkle said that I could put some of my pictures in his window. Perhaps I'll sell one to a rich old man one of these days.'

'I'm sure that you will,' said Delia.

That Saturday, she put fifteen dollars on the small table in the middle of their small **sitting room**.

sitting room a room in a house where people sit and talk

'Clementina's terrible,' she said. 'She never studies, never listens to me, and always wears white, which gets boring after a while. But the General's a nice, friendly man.'

Just then, Joe put eighteen dollars on the table.

'I sold a picture today to a fat man from Arizona,' he said. He saw it in Tinkle's window. He doesn't really understand art, but he wants another picture – of a train station – before he goes home.'

'Oh, I'm so happy that you didn't stop painting,' said Delia, 'And now we have thirty-three dollars. What a lot of money! We can have a really good dinner tonight.'

The next Saturday evening, Joe got home first. He put eighteen dollars on the table, and washed what looked like black paint from his hands.

Then Delia came home. Her hand had some white **cloth** around it, and her face was dark with worry.

cloth clothes are made of this

'What happened?' asked Joe.

'Oh, Clementina wanted a hot cheese sandwich in the middle of her lesson. Strange girl! Unluckily lots of hot cheese fell onto my hand and hurt it terribly. The General was very worried, and sent someone from downstairs to buy some things to put on it. But now it doesn't hurt so much.'

Then she saw Joe's money on the table.

'Did you sell another picture?'

'Yes, to the man from Arizona. But what time did you hurt your hand?'

'It was five o'clock when the **iron** . . . I mean, when the cheese burnt me.'

'Sit down, Delia,' said Joe kindly, 'And tell me where your money really comes from.'

Delia began crying. 'I couldn't find any music students,' she said. 'So I took a job in the big **laundry** on Twenty-Fourth Street. I told you stories about the General and Clementina to stop you feeling bad about my work. Then today, another girl at the laundry put a hot iron on my hand, and I thought of that hot cheese story on the way home. Please don't be angry. But how did you find out that my stories weren't true?'

'Well,' said Joe. 'At five o'clock I had to send up some **oil** and cloth for a woman in the laundry upstairs after she burnt her hand on an iron. I'm working downstairs in the **engine** room. I started there two weeks ago.'

'So you didn't really sell–'

'My buyer from Arizona, and your General Pinkney are both works of art – but not really music or painting.'

They both laughed.

'When you love your art, nothing–' began Joe.

But Delia put her hand over his mouth to stop him.

'No,' she said, 'It's just "When you love."'

iron a heavy metal thing that people use to make shirts and other clothes look good

laundry a place that washes people's clothes for them

oil a thick liquid that is sometimes used in medicines or to help machines to work

engine the machine in a laundry that makes it work

READING CHECK

Put the phrases in place in the summary of *The things we do for love.*

a a girl called Clementina

b and a cheese sandwich

c to pay for their classes

d in the same laundry

e from their art

f giving music classes

g and ~~get married~~

h but they need the money

i and is working in a laundry

and get married

Joe and Delia meet in New York [^ 1]. He's an artist and she's studying music. Sadly they soon don't have any money [^ 2]. One day Delia comes home happily and tells Joe that she has a job [^ 3]. She tells him about her student [^ 4]. Joe feels bad about her giving classes [^ 5]. The following Saturday Delia brings home fifteen dollars. Joe surprises her by putting eighteen dollars on the table and tells her that he has sold a painting. They both say that they are happy to be making money [^ 6]. The following Saturday Delia comes home with a bad hand and tells Joe a strange story about Clementina [^ 7]. Joe doesn't think that the story is true and starts to ask questions. In the end Delia tells him that she couldn't find any music students [^ 8], and Joe tells her that he is working [^ 9] too and that he couldn't sell any paintings. Neither of them told each other the truth because they didn't want to worry the other one.

WORD WORK

Use the words in the iron to complete the gaps in Delia's diary.

Dear Diary,

While I was working in the a) laundry this morning, one of the girls put a hot b)________ on my hand. It hurt terribly, and they gave me some c)______ to put on it.

All the way home I was thinking of a story to tell Joe. But how can you hurt your hand when you are giving a music lesson? I thought of a story about the d)____________'s daughter and a hot sandwich. When I got home, Joe was in the e)________________. I told him the story but he looked at the f)________ on my hand and asked what time I hurt my hand. It's so strange, but you see, Joe is working in the same g)___________, and he sent me the h)________ and the i)___________ from the j)______________ room where he works!

GUESS WHAT

Match the pictures and the descriptions of the characters from the next story.

☐ *Chunk McGowan*

☐ *Rosie*

☐ *Ikey Schoenstein*

☐ *Mr Riddle*

a is clever and hard-working but has no luck in love.

b is lazy and gets into a lot of fights.

c is unfriendly and loses something important.

d is pretty and can't decide what her true feelings are.

Story 5

Ikey Schoenstein's love-potion

The Blue Light **drugstore** was on the East Side of New York, near First Avenue. All the **medicines** there were made by hand. Ikey Schoenstein worked there at night. A thin, clever man, with a long nose and **glasses**, he was friendly to all who came for help when they were ill.

Ikey lived in a room in a house not far from the drugstore. His landlady was Mrs Riddle, and she had a daughter, Rosie. Ikey was deeply in love with Rosie, but he never told her about it. That was strange, because he was very good at talking to people in the drugstore.

There was another man living at Mrs Riddle's house who was in love with Rosie, too. His name was Chunk McGowan. Ikey had no hope of winning Rosie's love, but McGowan was very hopeful. He was also Ikey's friend. He often came to the drugstore, after a night fighting in the street, for something to put on a black eye or a cut.

One afternoon, he came hurriedly into the drugstore, and went straight to speak to his friend Ikey.

'I need some special medicine,' he said,

'Take off your coat,' said Ikey, 'And tell me where it hurts. Were you in a fight again? One of these days you'll get a knife in your back.'

'It wasn't a fight,' said McGowan, laughing. 'But you're right. It's under my coat that it hurts – in my **heart**. Ikey, Rosie and me are going to run away tonight to Harlem to get married.'

Ikey was mixing some medicine while he listened, and he tried not to drop it all on the floor.

McGowan's smiling face now looked worried.

'The thing is, we first thought of the plan two weeks ago.

drugstore a place that sells medicines

medicine something you eat or drink to make you get better when you are ill

glasses you wear these in front of your eyes to help you see better

heart the centre of feeling in someone; this is in your chest and it sends blood round your body

Sometimes Rosie says "yes" to it and sometimes "no". For the past two days she's said "yes", and we're hoping to leave in five hours' time. I don't want her to change her plans at the last minute.'

'And where does medicine come into it?' asked Ikey.

'Well, you see, old Mr Riddle doesn't like me. For a week now he's stopped Rosie coming out with me. I'm worried that she won't want to leave tonight because of him.

'Isn't there a medicine that you can give to a woman to make her like you better? I had a friend, Tim Lacy, who gave a **potion** like that to his girlfriend and they got married two weeks later. '

McGowan didn't notice Ikey's knowing smile at these words of his, and he went on.

'If I can just give a love-potion to Rosie at dinner tonight, I'm sure that she'll come with me.'

'And when are you running away?'

'Nine o'clock. Dinner's at seven. At eight, Rosie goes to bed with a bad head. At nine, I come round the back of the house and help her down the **fire escape** from her window. Then we're going straight to church, to get married.'

'We have to be careful about selling love-potions,' said Ikey. 'But because you're my friend, I'll make it for you, and you'll see how it changes the way Rosie thinks of you.'

Then he carefully made a sleeping-potion. It was sure to make anyone who took it sleep for a number of hours without waking up.

He gave the potion to his friend, telling him to put it into a drink if possible. McGowan thanked him, and left.

After that, Ikey sent a note to Mr Riddle, telling him about McGowan's plans.

Riddle came to the drugstore that afternoon. He was a strong, red-faced, angry man.

'Thanks for telling me, Ikey,' he said. 'That lazy, good-for-nothing Irishman. My room is just over Rosie's room. After dinner, I'll wait up there with my gun. If McGowan comes this evening, he'll go straight to the hospital – and not to church – tonight.'

potion something that you drink to make you feel better, love someone, or sleep

fire escape metal stairs outside the back or side of a building that you can escape down if there's a fire inside

'With Rosie asleep in her room, and old Riddle upstairs with his gun, McGowan's chances aren't looking good,' thought Ikey happily after Riddle left.

Next morning, at 8 o'clock, Ikey finished work and started walking to Mrs Riddle's house to learn the latest news. There in the street he met Chunk McGowan. McGowan shook Ikey's hand, and thanked him warmly.

'It worked,' he said, smiling. 'Rosie and me are now man and wife. You must come for dinner over at our place in Harlem some time soon.'

'But the potion?!' asked Ikey.

'Oh, that!' laughed McGowan. 'In the end I felt bad about questioning Rosie's love, but old Riddle was very unfriendly to me at dinner. It wasn't right for him to be so hard on the man who wanted to marry his daughter, I felt. So I put the potion in his coffee!'

READING CHECK

1 Join the sentence parts to tell the story of Ikey Schoenstein's love-potion.

a Mrs Riddle is	**1** in Mr Riddle's coffee.
b Ikey and Chunk	**2** Ikey and Chunk's landlady.
c Chunk and Rosie want	**3** to shoot Chunk.
d Chunk McGowan wants some medicine	**4** to send Rosie to sleep.
e Ikey doesn't do	**5** are both in love with Rosie.
f Ikey makes a sleeping potion	**6** to run away and get married.
g Ikey writes to Mr Riddle	**7** to make Rosie like him better.
h Mr Riddle plans	**8** to tell him about Chunk's plans.
i Chunk McGowan puts the potion	**9** that Chunk and Rosie are married.
j Ikey is surprised to hear	**10** what Chunk asks him to.

2 Who says what in the story? Tick the columns.

	Chunk	*Ikey*	*Mr Riddle*
a I need some special medicine.	☑	☐	☐
b Were you in a fight again?	☐	☐	☐
c Because you're my friend, I'll make it for you.	☐	☐	☐
d Thanks for telling me, Ikey.	☐	☐	☐
e McGowan will go straight to the hospital – and not to church – tonight.	☐	☐	☐
f Rosie and me are now man and wife.	☐	☐	☐

WORD WORK

Complete the puzzle to find the name of an island in New York City.

a It's the place where Ikey works.

b Chunk wants Ikey to make this for him for love.

c Ikey wears these because he can't see well.

d Chunk tells Ikey that this part of him hurts.

e Rosie climbs down this to run away with Chunk.

f Ikey's job is to make these by hand.

a			D	R	U	G	S	T	O	R	E	
b												
c												
d												
e												
f												

GUESS WHAT

Look at the pictures of the two main characters in the next story. Why do you think that Andy is interested in Miss Conway? Tick two boxes.

a ☐ He falls in love with her when he first sees her.

b ☐ She was married to a rich Italian man but he died.

c ☐ She is beautiful in black clothes.

d ☐ He wants to learn her secret.

e ☐ She lives in the same house as him and they see each other every day.

f ☐ He wants to marry her.

Story 6

The Count and the wedding guest

boarding house a small inexpensive hotel

introduce to bring people together for the first time by saying their names and something about them

guest a person that you invite to your home

cigar a thick brown cigarette

At dinner one night in the **boarding house** where Andy Donovan lived, near Second Avenue, his landlady **introduced** him to a new paying **guest** – Miss Conway.

'Nice to meet you, Mr Donovan,' said Miss Conway quietly, and then she went back to her meal.

She was an uninteresting young woman in a boring brown dress. Andy gave her a smile, and forgot her at once.

Two weeks later, Andy was smoking a **cigar** outside the front door when he heard someone coming out. He turned to see who it was, and was pleasantly surprised.

There was Miss Conway – all in black from her head to her feet. With her bright gold hair, her grey eyes, and her sad face, she looked lovely. **Mourning** clothes can make any woman look beautiful, and are sure to make any man look twice.

Andy immediately decided not to forget Miss Conway. He dropped his half-finished cigar on the ground and said, 'It's a fine evening, Miss Conway.'

'For those with the heart to enjoy it, Mr Donovan,' she replied sadly, looking down.

'I hope there hasn't been a death in the family,' he said.

'Not really in the family,' she replied. 'But I won't worry you with my troubles.'

'Worry me? But I'd really like to hear all about them Miss Conway. I mean, please feel free to speak to a true friend in your time of need.'

Miss Conway smiled sadly at this.

'I feel so lonely in New York,' she said. 'I have no friends here. But you have been kind to me, Mr Donovan. Thank you for that.'

It was true. Andy sometimes **passed** the salt to her at the dinner table.

'You're right,' he said. 'It's hard when you're alone. But why don't you take a walk in the **park**? That'll make you feel better, I'm sure. I'll go along with you if you want.'

'Thank you, Mr Donovan. I'd like that. If you're happy to take a walk with someone like me who has a sad and heavy heart.'

'He was my **fiancé**,' said Miss Conway after an hour in the park. 'We wanted to get married. He was a real Italian Count, with a big old house in Italy. **Count** Fernando Mazzini was his name, and he was a great dresser. Father didn't agree to it, of course. When we ran away together, he came after us and found us.

mourning black clothes that people wear for a time after someone in their family or a good friend has died

pass to give something to someone when they need it

park a big garden that is open to everybody to visit

fiancé the man that a woman is going to marry

Count an important man

'In the end, when he learned how rich Fernando was, father agreed to a spring **wedding**. Fernando wanted to give me a wedding present of seven thousand dollars – for the dress, the flowers, the dinner and all. But father was **proud** and said "no". So when the Count went back to Italy to get his big old house ready for us, I got myself a job in a **candy store** to help pay for the wedding.

'Then three days ago, I got a letter from Italy, saying that Fernando was dead. It was a terrible **gondola** accident that killed him they said.

'So that explains my mourning, Mr Donovan. I'll never forget Fernando, you see. And after losing him, I'm afraid I just can't look at any other man.'

'I'm really sorry for you,' said Andy. 'And I'm your true friend. I want you to know that.'

'I have his picture here in my **locket**,' said Miss Conway tearfully. 'And because you're a true friend, Mr Donovan, I'll show it to you.'

For some time Andy studied the photograph in the locket that Miss Conway opened for him. The man's face was young, bright and clever. It was the face of a strong man that other people are always ready to follow.

'I have a larger photograph in my room,' said Miss Conway. 'I'll show you later. They're the only things that I have of Fernando now. But he'll always be in my heart.'

Andy decided there and then to try to win Miss Conway's heart from the Count. He took her to have an ice cream, but her grey eyes still looked sad.

That evening, she brought down the larger photograph and showed it to Andy. He looked at it silently.

'He gave this to me the night that he left for Italy,' said Miss Conway.

'A fine-looking man,' said Andy. 'Now would you like to come out with me again next Sunday afternoon?'

wedding the day when two people marry

proud not wanting help from other people

candy sweet food made of sugar or chocolate

store a shop

gondola you can go across the water in this in Venice

locket a small, flat, gold or silver box that you wear around your neck, usually with a photograph of someone that you love inside it

A month later, they told the landlady and the other guests at the boarding house of their plans to get married. Miss Conway stayed in mourning.

A week after that, they were sitting in the park near the boarding house. Andy's usually smiling face was dark with worry, and he was strangely silent.

'What's the matter, Andy?' asked Miss Conway.

'Well, you've heard of Big Mike Sullivan, haven't you?' said Andy, after a while.

'No, I haven't. Who is he?'

'He's a great New York **politician**, and a friend of mine. I met him today, and he wants to come to our wedding. I'd really like him to come.'

'OK. So he can be our guest.'

'Right, but before we can have our wedding I need to know something. Do you still prefer Count Mazzini over me?'

Suddenly Miss Conway started crying.

'Oh, Andy, there never was a Count. All the other girls had boyfriends – but I didn't. And you know how good I look in black. So I bought a big photograph of a man that I didn't know at a photograph store, and got a small one, too, for my locket. Then I thought up the story of the Count's death and put on my black clothes. I'm just a big **fake**. And now you won't marry me because of it, I'm sure. And you're the only man that I've ever loved!'

Smiling, Andy took her in his arms.

'Do you still want to marry me after what I've done?' she asked in surprise.

'Of course,' he replied. 'You were very good to explain it all to me. Now we can forget the Count, there's nothing to stop us becoming man and wife.'

'Andy,' Miss Conway went on, 'Did you really think that my stories about the Count were true?'

'Not really,' he replied, taking out a cigar, 'Mostly because that photograph in your locket is of my friend Mike Sullivan.'

politician a person who helps to make laws in a country

fake not real

READING CHECK

Complete the sentences about *The Count and the wedding guest* in the best way.

a Andy is interested in Miss Conway when he meets her for *the first time / the second time / dinner.*

b The next time that Andy sees Miss Conway he *gives her the salt / asks her to marry him / is more interested in her.*

c Miss Conway wears black because *it's a good colour for her / she's sad / her boyfriend died.*

d She tells Andy that her boyfriend was an Italian Count but that *her father didn't like him / he has left her and gone back to Italy / he has just died.*

e She cries because *she thinks that Andy won't love her when she tells him the true story / Andy wants Mike Sullivan at the wedding / she still loves the Count.*

f Andy knows from the start that the Count isn't real because *Miss Conway tells him the true story / the story is strange / her photos are of his friend.*

g Miss Conway tells the story about the Count because she *isn't in love with Andy / wants to be more interesting to Andy / has no friends in New York.*

WORD WORK

1 Unjumble the letters to label the pictures.

a d a c n y

candy

b g r a i c

_ _ _ _ _

c d l o o a n g

_ _ _ _ _ _ _

d t o l e c k

_ _ _ _ _ _

e k a r p

_ _ _ _

f t r o s e

_ _ _ _ _

g d w i g e n d

_ _ _ _ _ _ _

h g n r u m o i n

_ _ _ _ _ _ _ _

ACTIVITIES

2 Find words around the cake from *The Count and the wedding guest*.

3 Match the words in Activity 2 with the definitions.

a Andy and Miss Conway live in this. a boarding house

b Mike Sullivan's job. a __________

c The landlady decides to do this to Andy and Miss Conway. __________

d Miss Conway says that her boyfriend was this. a _____

e In the end, Miss Conway tells Andy that she is this. a ____

f When you're going to get married, your boyfriend is this. your ______

g Mike Sullivan wants to be this at the wedding. a _____

h Miss Conway says that her father didn't want money from the count because he was this. _____

GUESS WHAT

The next story is about this man. Which four things do you think that you will read about?

a ☐ a menu

b ☐ some bottles of medicine

c ☐ a fur coat

d ☐ some handcuffs

e ☐ a fake doctor

f ☐ a crown

g ☐ a typewriter

h ☐ $250

Story 7

Thinking yourself rich

My real name's Jeff Peters. But when I visited Fisher Hill, **Arkansas**, I went there as Doctor **Waugh-Hoo**, the famous **Indian** medicine man.

I had only five dollars in my pocket, so I got fifty medicine bottles from the drugstore, and went straight to my hotel room. The other things that I needed were in my bag.

At the hotel I put water, purple colouring, and a little Chinchona – real medicine that comes from a Peruvian tree – into every bottle. Then I put **labels** on them saying: 'DR WAUGH-HOO'S INDIAN POTION – SURE TO BRING THE DEAD TO LIFE!' I was ready for business.

I started that night on a street in the centre of town. After selling twenty-five bottles at twenty cents each, I felt a hand on my arm. It was a policeman.

'Do you have a **licence** to sell medicine here?' he asked.

'No, I don't.' I replied.

'Well, you'll have to stop, then.'

I stopped, went back to my hotel at once, and spoke to the **landlord**.

'You'll never get a licence,' he said. 'Doctor Hoskins is the only doctor here, and his wife's the Mayor's sister. A fake doctor has no chance.'

'I'm not a doctor. I'm a travelling **salesman**. And I'll get a licence tomorrow.'

I went to the Mayor's office early the next day, but he wasn't there. So I went back to my hotel, sat in a chair, had a smoke, and waited.

Soon a young man in a blue suit sat down next to me and asked me the time.

'It's ten o'clock,' I said, 'And you're Andy Tucker.

Arkansas /ˈɑːkənˌsɔː/

Waugh-Hoo /ˈwa ˌhuː/

Indian a person who lived in America before white people arrived

label a piece of paper or cloth that you fix to something to give information about it

licence an important paper that says you can do something

landlord a man who has a hotel

salesman someone who sells things

I remember you.'

Andy was a good street salesman, and I needed a **partner**. So we agreed to go outside.

He was just off the train, and had plans to ask people in Fisher Hill for money to build a new bath house at Eureka **Springs**. I told him how things were in Fisher Hill, and we sat and talked.

Next morning, at eleven o'clock, an old black man came looking for me at the hotel, where I sat alone.

'You must come, sir,' he said. 'The Mayor's terribly ill. He needs your help.'

'Get Dr Hoskins,' I replied.

'He can't come, **sir**. He's in the country. But the Mayor's nearly dying. He needs help right now!'

'OK,' I said, 'I can't leave a man in need. I'll come.'

When I arrived, I found the Mayor in bed, looking bad. A young man stood near him holding a cup of water.

partner someone to work with

spring a place where water comes up from under the ground

sir when you are speaking to a man that you do not know well, or who is more important than you, you call him this

'Doctor, can you help me? It's terrible,' said the Mayor.

'Well, I'm not here as a doctor,' I said, 'but as a friend.'

'Thank you, Doctor Waugh-hoo,' he replied. 'This young man is my **nephew**, Mr Biddle. He's tried to help, but it's no good. Ooooh, it hurts!'

I **nodded** at Biddle, and sat on the bed. I looked at the Mayor's eyes, tongue and ears, and listened to his heart and chest.

'What's the matter with me?' he asked.

'Mr Mayor,' I said, 'I'm sorry to say that you have a dangerous pneumonia of the circular dandelion in the upper right vegetable of your heart.'

'Can you give me something for it?'

'Medicine won't touch it, I'm afraid,' I said. 'Your only hope is **hypnosis**!'

'Hypno- what?' said the Mayor.

'It means me helping you to think yourself well again,' I explained helpfully.

'Can you do that?' asked the Mayor.

'Well, I'm not a doctor, you understand, but to save your life I'm more than ready to do some hypnosis on you – if you forget the licence question.'

'Of course,' he said. 'And please can you start now. It's hurting a lot!'

'Hypnosis costs two hundred and fifty dollars for two visits,' I said.

'That's not much to pay for my life,' said the Mayor.

So I began. Looking him in the eye, I said: 'Look into my eyes. You're sleepy. Your upper right vegetable isn't hurting now. The circular dandelion's going. You have no upper right vegetable, no heart, no body. Your eyes are closing.'

I left him sleeping and went back to the hotel. The next day I went back to his house early.

'How is he?' I asked Mr Biddle at the bedroom door.

nephew your sister's (or brother's) son

nod to move your head up and down

hypnosis using your voice to make someone sleep and in that sleep telling them to change the way that they think or what they do when they wake up

'A lot better,' said the young man.

I did some more hypnosis on the Mayor, and he said that nothing hurt him after that.

'Stay in bed, rest for two days, and you'll be fine. You were very lucky that I was in town yesterday,' I said. 'And now for my money.'

'Here it is,' said the Mayor, taking the bills from the table by his bed and giving them to me. 'And put your name on this,' he went on, giving me a paper that said:

For two visits by Dr Waugh-Hoo
to the Mayor of Fisher Hill
Two hundred and fifty dollars

____

I wrote *Dr Waugh-Hoo* at the bottom of the paper and gave it back to him.

'Now do your work, officer,' said the Mayor with a big smile on his face. Suddenly he didn't look ill at all.

Mr Biddle put his hand on my arm.

'I **arrest** you Dr Waugh-Hoo – or Jeff Peters, to give you your usual name – for selling fake medicine without a licence,' he said.

'Who are you?' I cried.

'He's a detective,' said the Mayor, 'working for the Arkansas **Medical Society**. He's followed you all over Arkansas for weeks. He came to me yesterday, and told me all about you, and we made a plan to catch you. You won't sell your fake medicine around here any more.'

'A detective!' I said.

'That's right. And now we're going to see the **sheriff**,' said the young man.

arrest to take a person to prison

medical society a group of the most important doctors in a place that decides which medicines people can sell and who are bad doctors

sheriff a person who looks after the law in a town in the USA

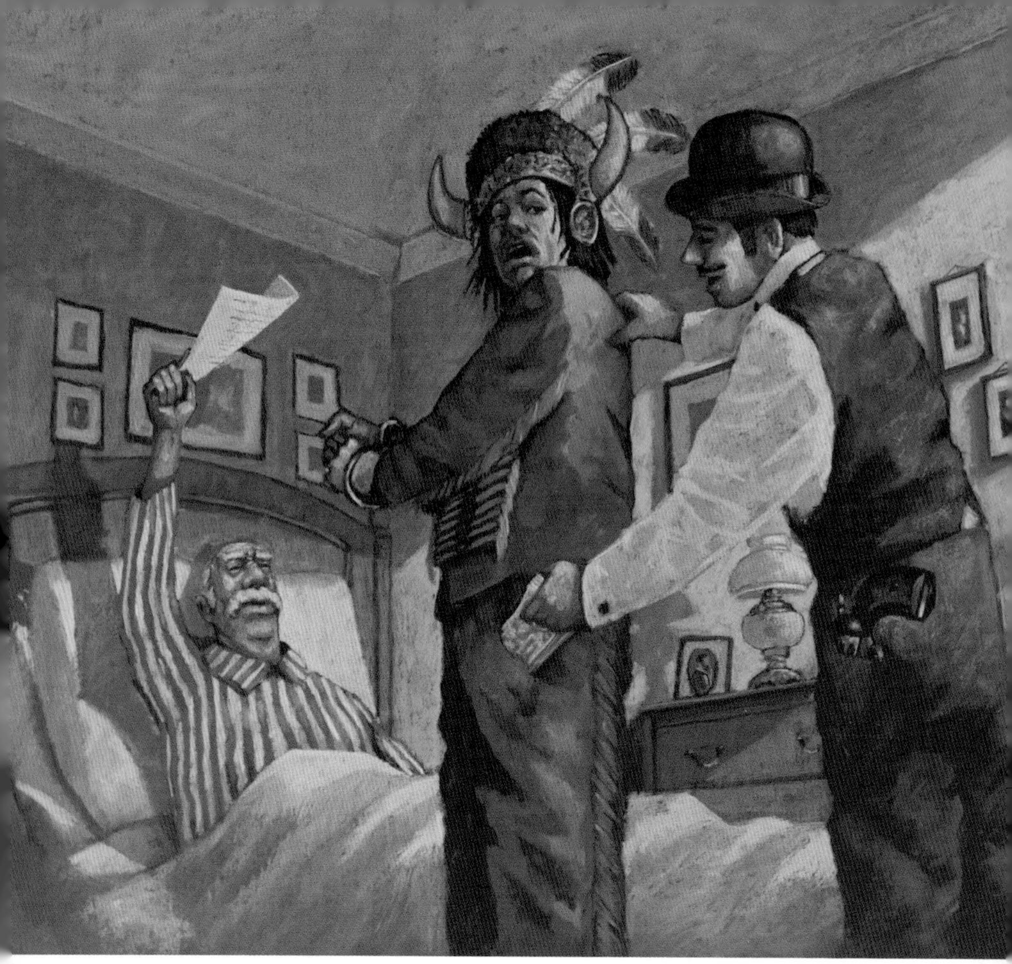

'Oh, no we're not,' I cried, taking his neck in my hands and nearly pushing him through the window.

Then he pulled out a gun, and put it to my head. I stood still. After that, he put handcuffs on me, and took the money out of my pocket.

'I'll need to take this to the sheriff, sir. I'll be sure to tell him that these were your bills with my marks on them. You'll get it all back once the criminal is in jail.'

'That's fine by me, Mr Biddle,' said the Mayor. Then he turned to me, laughing. 'Well Dr Waugh-hoo. Show us your famous hypnosis now. Make those handcuffs go away by thinking yourself free again!'

'Come on, officer,' I said. 'I'll go quietly.'

At the door, I shook my handcuffs at the Mayor, saying, 'The time will come when you understand that hypnosis works, and that it worked very well for me here today, too.'

And in a way that was true. When we arrived out on the street, I said to Mr Biddle, 'Somebody could see us. Take the handcuffs off now, Andy.' And he did.

Biddle was really my old friend Andy Tucker, you see, and it was all his **idea**. And that's how we started in business together.

idea something that you think

READING CHECK

Put these sentences in the correct order. Number them 1 – 10.

- **a** ☐ The Mayor introduces Peters to Mr Biddle.
- **b** ☐ Mr Biddle arrests Peters when he writes his name on a bill.
- **c** ☐ A policeman stops Peters selling medicine in the street.
- **d** ☐ Jeff Peters and Andy Tucker walk away from the Mayor's house together.
- **e** 1 Jeff Peters arrives in Fisher Hill and dresses as Dr Waugh-Hoo.
- **f** ☐ A man goes to the hotel where Peters is staying and asks him to help the Mayor.
- **g** ☐ The next day Peters goes back to see the Mayor and asks for his money.
- **h** ☐ The Mayor thinks that Mr Biddle is taking Dr Waugh-Hoo to jail.
- **i** ☐ Peters looks at the Mayor and uses some stupid words to explain why he is ill.
- **j** ☐ Peters meets Andy Tucker and they make plans together.

WORD WORK

Replace the orange phrases with words from *Thinking yourself rich*.

- **a** It was Andy Tucker's **interesting thought** to say that he was a detective. idea
- **b** The **piece of paper** on the bottle says that the medicine will bring the dead to life. _ _ _ _ _
- **c** My **brother's son** is staying with me for a few days. _ _ _ _ _ _
- **d** The Mayor wants Mr Biddle to **take** Dr Waugh-Hoo **to jail**. _ _ _ _ _ _
- **e** Peters needs a **paper saying that it's OK for him** to sell his medicine in Fisher Hill. _ _ _ _ _ _ _
- **f** There's a **place where water comes out of the ground** in the field behind our house. _ _ _ _ _ _
- **g** My father is a **person who sells things** and he travels a lot. _ _ _ _ _ _ _ _
- **h** I need a **person to work with** to help me with my new business. _ _ _ _ _ _ _
- **i** Don't say anything, just **move your head up and down** when I tell you the right answer. _ _ _
- **j** They say that **telling people what to do when they are nearly asleep** is a good way to stop smoking. _ _ _ _ _ _ _ _

GUESS WHAT

What happens in the next story – *Lost and found*? Complete the four sentences with the words from the wheel below.

a Helen loses her . . . . on the day of her wedding.

b Her . . . . stops her from looking for love with another man.

c Many years later she suddenly finds her . . . . in her house.

d Helen's . . . . isn't a very important thing in her life. She just wants to be happy.

Helen at 18

Story 8

Lost and found

Near Abingdon Square there was a house with a small store selling **stationery** on the ground floor. Both the house and the store belonged to old Mrs Mayo.

One night twenty years ago, there was a wedding in the rooms over the store. Helen, Mrs Mayo's daughter, married Frank Barry. Frank's best friend, John Delaney, was the **best man**. Helen was only eighteen at the time, and before the wedding both Frank and John were in love with her. But when Frank won her heart, John shook his friend's hand and said '**congratulations**'.

After the wedding, Helen ran upstairs to put on her hat. She and Frank were leaving for a week's **honeymoon** in Virginia that same night. The rest of the wedding party were still downstairs.

Suddenly she heard someone running up the fire escape, and John Delaney jumped into the room.

'Come away with me tonight,' he cried. 'I love you!'

'What do you mean speaking to me like that? I'm a married woman!' said Helen coldly.

'I can't help it. I love you. I'll always love you.'

'Go back down the fire escape this minute!'

'If you won't have me, I'll travel the world. I'll go to Africa and try to forget you.'

'Get out,' said Helen, 'before someone comes in.'

John knelt on the floor in front of her, and she gave him her hand to kiss.

Just then, Frank walked in, worrying why Helen was taking so long to put on her hat.

John kissed Helen's hand, and ran out of the room and down the fire escape to Africa.

stationery paper, pens, pencils and other things for the office

best man a man at a wedding who helps the man that is getting married

congratulations well done

honeymoon a holiday that a man and a woman take together just after they get married

'What was all that about?' shouted Frank.

Helen went to him, and tried to explain – but it was no good. Frank threw her to the floor, saying, 'I never want to see you again!' Then he ran downstairs, past the surprised wedding guests, and out into the night.

When Mrs Mayo died, her daughter, Helen Barry, **inherited** the store and the house. Twenty years after her wedding, Mrs Barry was still beautiful.

Because business in the store wasn't good, Mrs Barry decided to take paying guests upstairs. Two large rooms on the third floor were made ready for them, one at the front of the house and one at the back.

inherit to get something as a present from someone when they die

One day a musician arrived and took the front room. His name was Ramonti. He played the **violin**, and was looking for a quiet place to live.

He had a fine head of grey hair, and his face – with its short, **foreign**-looking beard – still looked young. He was friendly, and Mrs Barry enjoyed having him in the house.

She had a comfortable room for herself – half office and half sitting room – on the first floor. Here she wrote her business letters at her desk during the day, or sat and read in the evening by a warm fire. Ramonti often visited her there – telling her all about his time as a poor young music student in Paris many years before, when he studied with a world famous violinist.

Mrs Barry's second paying guest was a good-looking man in his early forties. He had a brown beard, and strangely sad eyes. He also liked spending time with Mrs Barry, and telling her about his travels. There was a mystery about this man that Mrs Barry found most interesting. His voice made her remember her first love, all those years ago. Soon she felt sure that he belonged, in some way, to that past story. In the end, she decided – in the way that women have – that this man was her husband of long ago. She saw the love in his eyes. But she said nothing to him about it. After all, a husband who leaves home on his wedding night for twenty years can't hope to find his wife waiting for him with open arms when he comes back.

One evening, Ramonti came to speak to Helen.

'I love you, and want to marry you,' he told her. 'But before you say anything, I must tell you that my **manager** gave me the name "Ramonti". I don't really know who I am or where I come from. The first thing that I remember in my life is waking up as a young man in a hospital. I know nothing of what happened before then. They told me that I hit my head badly on the ground in the street one night,

violin a musical instrument, made of wood with strings across it

foreign not from your country

manager a person who organizes the work of musicians, singers and other artists

and that an ambulance brought me to the hospital. No one knew who I was. After I left the hospital, I started playing the violin, and now I'm a famous musician. But Mrs Barry, the first time that I saw you, I knew that you were the only woman in the world for me.'

Helen felt young again, and very happy, while she looked into Ramonti's eyes. Her heart was full of love for the violinist, which came as a great surprise to her.

'Mr Ramonti,' she said quickly, 'I'm sorry, but I must ask you to stop. You see, I'm a married woman.'

Then she told him the sad story of her life. After that, Ramonti took her hand, kissed it softly, and went up to his room slowly.

Helen looked sadly down at her hand. Two kisses on it, and only two lovers' goodbyes for her to remember. It was really just too bad for words.

Later that evening, her other paying guest came to speak to her. He also said that he loved her.

'Helen, don't you remember me?' he cried. 'I thought that I saw it in your eyes. Can you forget the past, and remember the love that has lasted for twenty years? I've been so bad to you. I was afraid to come back. But my love was stronger. Can you **forgive** me?'

Helen didn't know what to do. Half her heart was full of her old love for her husband. But a newer, stronger love filled the other half. And both loves fought against each other.

Just then, she heard soft, sad, sweet violin music coming from upstairs. The music and the musician called her, but 'doing the right thing' stopped her from going.

'Forgive me,' said the man at her side.

'Twenty years is a long time to stay away from the woman that you say you love.'

'But I wasn't sure!' he cried. 'Look, I'll tell you everything. That night when he left, I went after him. I didn't know what I was doing. On a dark street I knocked him down and he didn't get up again. There was blood on his head from where it hit the hard ground. I didn't mean to kill him. I hid not far away, and saw an ambulance come for him. I know that you married him Helen, but–'

'Who *are* you?' cried the woman in surprise.

'Don't you remember me, Helen. I'm the one that always loved you the best. I'm John Delaney. Can you forgive–'

But she was far away, hurrying upstairs towards the music, towards the man who didn't remember, but who knew that she was the one for him in each of his two lives. And, running lightly up those long stairs, she called him by his old name: 'Frank, Frank! Frank!'

forgive (*past* **forgave**, **forgiven**) to stop being angry with someone for something bad that they did

READING CHECK

1 What happened twenty years before the story starts? Join the sentence parts.

- **a** Helen Mayo and Frank Barry
- **b** Frank's best friend, John Delaney
- **c** After the wedding Frank saw
- **d** Both of the men ran away
- **e** John Delaney waited for Frank
- **f** Frank woke up in a hospital
- **g** After Frank left the hospital
- **h** John Delaney ran away and

1. he started playing the violin.
2. and knocked him down in the street.
3. travelled the world.
4. and Helen didn't see them again.
5. got married.
6. but he didn't remember anything.
7. John kissing Helen's hand.
8. was also in love with Helen.

2 Tick the correct person for the gaps.

- **a** . . . decides to take paying guests because she needs the money.

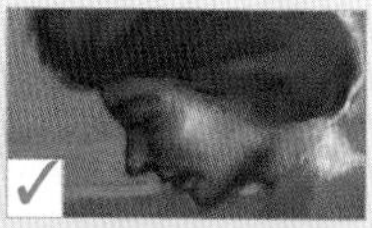

- **b** Mrs Barry enjoys talking to . . . about his years as a student.

- **c** . . . tells Helen about his world travels.

- **d** Helen decides that . . . is her husband of long ago.

- **e** When . . . tells Helen he loves her, she knows she's also in love with him.

- **f** When the other guest tells her his story she understands that he was . . . .

- **g** Helen runs up the stairs to see . . . .

ACTIVITIES

WORD WORK

Tick the pictures to answer the questions.

a Which of these is stationery?

b Which of these is a best man?

c When do you say 'Congratulations!'?

d Who will soon be on honeymoon?

e What do people often inherit?

f Which person has a manager?

g Who is someone forgiving someone?

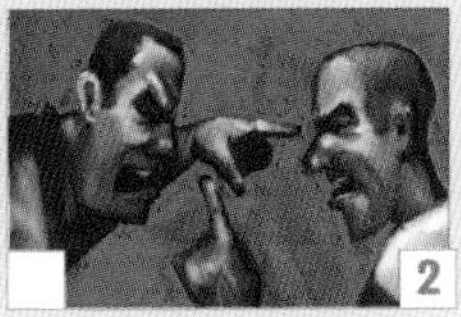

Project A *History Quiz*

1 Do the history quiz with a partner.

History Quiz: the USA from 1900–1910

1 Who was the US President at the start of 1901 and what happened to him?

a It was President McKinley and someone shot him dead.

b It was President Bush and he got married.

c It was George Washington and he left the White House that year.

2 What happened at Kitty Hawk in 1903?

a The first plane crossed the Atlantic.

b The first plane flew in the sky.

c The Wright brothers opened a bicycle shop.

3 Where was the earthquake that knocked city buildings to the ground and killed more than 2,500 people in 1906?

a San Francisco.

b Washington D.C.

c New York.

4 In 1901 Teddy Roosevelt became President. What was his job before that?

a He made things for children to play with.

b He had a farm with cows on it in the West.

c He was a train driver.

5 What did Henry Ford start doing in 1903?

a Sending sounds by radio across the Atlantic.

b Making films.

c Selling cars.

6 What opened in New York in 1904?

a The first subway lines.

b The Empire State Building.

c The Statue of Liberty.

2 Choose an important decade in the history of your country and make notes about those ten years.

Daily Life:

Free Time:

Famous people:

Inventions:

Important things that happened:

3 Write a quiz about the decade that you chose. Use the questions in the USA quiz and your notes to help you.

4 Give your quiz to one of your classmates to do.

Project B *Film Scenes*

1 Look at the New York photo. Imagine it's the background for a scene in a film of an O. Henry story. Which stories in this book have New York street scenes?

- [ ] Fine furs for a lady
- [ ] Springtime on the menu
- [ ] The last leaf
- [ ] The things we do for love
- [ ] Ikey Schoenstein's love-potion
- [ ] The Count and the wedding guest
- [ ] Thinking yourself rich
- [ ] Lost and found

2 Read a description of the scene and complete the table. Which story is it from? Find the pages and lines in this book that it describes.

Which story is it from?	
Which page does it match?	
Which lines does it describe?	

A young man and woman are walking down (**a**) a busy street together. There are some horses and carts (**b**). There are lots of people (**c**) in the street, too. Near the young couple, (**d**), there are some market stalls selling fruit and vegetables. It's a poor part of town.

The couple are walking along (**e**). He's wearing a brown suit, a white shirt, and a brown hat. She's wearing a long skirt and some furs around her neck (**f**). (**g**) the people in the street stop and look at them and talk about them.

A police detective is on the same side of the street (**h**) behind the couple. He's wearing a grey suit (**i**). He sees that something is happening (**j**) and starts walking faster. On his way, he stops and questions a man (**k**). When he catches up with the couple, he touches the man's arm with his hand and asks him something. The man turns to the detective (**l**). The woman turns to look at the man (**m**).

3 The words and phrases below add more detail to the description. Match them with the letters (a) to (m).

about 50 metres	☐	and she's really happy	☐
and he has serious eyes	☐	angrily	☐
arm in arm	☐	When they walk past,	☐
at the side of the road	☐	going up and down the street	☐
in front of him	☐	young and old	☐
standing on a corner	☐	the left-hand side of	☐
with worried eyes	☐		

4 Choose a scene from a different story in this book. Make notes to answer these questions. Use the photos to help you to 'see' the scene in your head.

- **a** Is the scene inside or outside?
- **b** Some key words to describe the scene:
- **c** How many of the story characters are in the scene?
- **d** Are there any other people in the background?
- **e** What are the different people wearing?
- **f** What are they doing?

5 Write a description of your scene. Exchange it with a partner. Read your partner's description. Find the story, the pages, and the lines in this book that it describes.

GRAMMAR CHECK

Non-defining relative clauses with who and which

We can use non-defining relative clauses to give more information about a person or thing.

We use who to start a non-defining relative clause about a person.

Kid Brady, who was in a criminal gang, fell in love with Molly McKeever.

We use which to start a non-defining relative clause about a thing.

His gang worked between Eleventh and Twelfth Avenues, which are in the west of New York.

We use commas to separate non-defining relative clauses from the main sentence.

1 Rewrite each pair of sentences as one sentence with a non-defining relative clause.

a Molly didn't like Brady being a criminal. She was a good woman.

Molly, who was a good woman, didn't like Brady being a criminal.

b So Brady started working as a plumber. This made Molly happy.

……………………………………………………………

c Brady gave Molly a strange parcel one day. It had furs in it.

……………………………………………………………

d Brady asked Molly to go for a walk in the street. He was feeling very happy.

……………………………………………………………

e Ransom started asking questions. He saw that people in the street were excited by something.

……………………………………………………………

f One man said that Molly was wearing expensive Russian furs. He was standing on a street corner.

……………………………………………………………

g A plumber's pay isn't enough to buy $900 furs. It's $75 a month.

……………………………………………………………

h Mrs Hethcote said that her furs were gone. She lived on West Seventh Street.

……………………………………………………………

i Kohen knew that Molly's furs weren't expensive. He sold furs when he was younger.

……………………………………………………………

GRAMMAR CHECK

Past Continuous and Past Simple with when and while

We use the Past Continuous for a longer activity in the past, and the Past Simple for a shorter action that happens in the middle of that first activity.

Sara was typing menus when she saw the word 'dandelion'.

The word while often goes before the Past Continuous verb and when before the Past Simple verb.

While she was staying at Sunnybrook Farm, she met Walter Franklin.

We put a comma after the when or while clause if it comes first in the sentence.

2 Complete these sentences with the Past Continuous or Past Simple form of the verbs in brackets.

a While Sarah ...was sitting... (sit) under a tree, Walter ...made... (make) her a crown of dandelion flowers.

b They .... (walk) back to the farm when Walter .... (say) that he wanted to marry her.

c While Sarah .... (look) out of her window, she .... (not see) the factory opposite.

d When the waiter from Schulenberg's restaurant .... (knock) on Sarah's door, she .... (remember) her holiday in the country.

e Sarah .... (have) no more news from Walter while she .... (work) back in New York.

f There .... (be) a ring at the front door while Sarah .... (read) her book.

g While Sarah .... (listen), she .... (hear) a man's voice downstairs.

h While Walter .... (run) upstairs, Sarah .... (open) her room door.

i Walter .... (read) Schulenberg's menu when he .... (see) his name on it.

GRAMMAR CHECK

Making offers and suggestions with let's, shall, and would like

We can make suggestions with let's (let us) + infinitive without to.

Let's eat at that restaurant on Eighth Street.

We can also make suggestions with Would you like...? + noun phrase/infinitive with to or Shall we...? + infinitive without to.

Would you like some Italian food?

Would you like to live in Greenwich Village?

Shall we take the top floor of a house together?

We can make offers with Shall I...? + infinitive without to.

Shall I call the doctor?

3 Complete the conversation between Joanna and Sue with *Let's*, *Shall I/we*, or *Would you like*.

Joanna: Oh, you're not asleep. a) ..Shall.. I sit with you?

Sue: Don't worry about me.

Joanna: b) .... some soup?

Sue: No, thank you.

Joanna: c) .... take the soup away?

Sue: Yes, please. When that last ivy leaf falls I'm going to die, you know.

Joanna: Don't say that. d).................... think of nice things. e).................... go to Naples together next spring?

Sue: You can. I'm not going to be alive then.

Joanna: Don't talk like that. f).................... close the blind for you?

Sue: No. Please leave it open.

Joanna: g).................... to rest?

Sue: Yes.

GRAMMAR

GRAMMAR CHECK

Direct and reported speech

In direct speech we give the words that people say.	In reported speech we put the verb one step into the past and change the personal pronouns and possessive adjectives.
'I'll give music lessons to get some more money,' said Delia.	*Delia said that she would give music lessons to get some more money.*
'You can put some pictures in my window,' said Tinkle to Joe.	*Tinkle said that Joe could put some pictures in his window.*

Time phrases like today and this week become that day, that week in reported speech, too.

4 Rewrite these direct speech sentences as reported speech.

a 'The Pinkneys live in a big house,' said Delia.

Delia said that the Pinkneys lived in a big house.

b 'I can't let you do all the work,' said Joe to Delia.

....

c 'I really don't like you giving lessons,' said Joe to Delia.

....

d 'Perhaps I'll sell a picture to a rich old man,' said Joe.

....

e 'Clementina never listens to me, and always wears white,' said Delia.

....

f 'A buyer from Arizona wants a picture of a train station by the end of this week,' said Joe.

....

g 'We have thirty-three dollars. So we can have a really good dinner tonight,' said Delia to Joe.

....

h 'My hand doesn't hurt this evening,' said Delia.

....

i 'My buyer from Arizona and your General Pinkney are both works of art,' said Joe to Delia.

....

GRAMMAR

GRAMMAR CHECK

Present Perfect Simple + for/since or already/yet

We make the Present Perfect Simple with have/has + the past participle. We can use it to talk about something that started in the past and continues now.

The Blue Light drugstore has been here for years.

I've lived at the Riddles' house since I came to New York.

We use for to talk about a period of time and since to talk about a past point in time.

We can also use the Present Perfect Simple to talk about something that happened at some time in the past without saying when.

We can use the adverbs already and not yet in this kind of Present Perfect Simple sentence.

We've been to the church already. (= earlier than you think usual)

We haven't told Rosie's mother and father yet. (= later than you think usual)

5 Complete the sentences with *for*, *since*, *already*, or *yet*.

- **a** Chunk's known Rosie Riddle ..for.. some weeks.
- **b** I've helped Chunk .... he arrived at the Riddles' house.
- **c** I've given Chunk the sleeping-potion ....
- **d** Chunk hasn't given the sleeping-potion to Rosie ....
- **e** I've spoken to Mr Riddle about Chunk's plans ....
- **f** I've loved Rosie myself .... many months.

6 Complete the text with the Present Perfect form of the verbs in brackets.

a) ..I've Known.. (I/know) Andy Donovan for nearly two months. b) .... (we/have) lots of walks together in the park, and c) .... (we/talk) a lot. d) .... (he/take) me out for an ice cream a number of times. e) .... (I/wear) black since we met. You see, f) .... (I/be) in mourning since my fiancé, Count Fernando Mazzini, died in a gondola accident seven weeks ago. That's the story g) .... (Andy/hear), at least! Now h) .... (Andy/ask) me to marry him. i) .... (he/buy) me a ring already! But j) .... (we/not/decide) about who to invite to the wedding yet. How can I tell him now that the story of the Count isn't true?

GRAMMAR CHECK

Going to Future: intentions and predictions

We make the going to future with the verb be + going to + infinitive.

We can use the going to future for intentions.

We're going to make some money.

We can also use the going to future for predictions.

The mayor isn't going to be very happy when he finds out.

7 Complete these sentences with the *going to* future form of the verbs in brackets.

- **a** We're going to visit (we/visit) the Mayor of Fisher Hill. [I]
- **b** .... (I/tell) him that I'm a detective. [ ]
- **c** .... (I/say) that I want to catch you. [ ]
- **d** .... (he/believe) me. [ ]
- **e** .... (he/ask) you to help him. [ ]
- **f** .... (I/use) hypnosis on him. [ ]
- **g** .... (he/pay) me two hundred and fifty dollars. [ ]
- **h** .... (I/write) my name on the paper that he gives me. [ ]
- **i** .... (I/arrest) you. [ ]
- **j** .... (I/put) the money in my pocket. [ ]
- **k** .... (we/leave) his house together. [ ]
- **l** .... (it/not/be) difficult. [ ]
- **m** .... (we/go) take the next train out of Fisher Hill. [ ]

8 Which sentences in exercise 7 are intentions and which are predictions? Mark them I for intentions or P for predictions.

GRAMMAR CHECK

That clauses after forget, hear, know, remember, and think

After the verbs forget, hear, know, remember and think we can use that + a clause **(subject + verb + the rest of a sentence).**

Helen forgot that she was sad when she spoke to Ramonti.

John didn't hear that Frank was still alive.

John knew that Helen was a married woman.

Ramonti didn't remember that his name was really Frank Barry.

John thought that Helen would forgive him.

9 Match the sentence halves correctly. Put the numbers in the boxes.

a Frank didn't know that [4]
b Ramonti remembered that [ ]
c Ramonti heard that [ ]
d Ramonti forgot that [ ]
e Helen thought that [ ]
f John knew that [ ]
g John thought that [ ]
h Helen heard that [ ]
i Helen knew that [ ]

1 he had a bad accident before they took him to the hospital.
2 he was Helen's husband years before.
3 he first woke up, knowing nothing, in a hospital.
4 ~~Helen didn't want John in her room on her wedding night.~~
5 it was wrong of him to knock Frank down in the street.
6 her other paying guest was her husband.
7 her other paying guest was John Delaney.
8 she loved her husband, the musician, best.
9 he was Frank Barry's murderer.

DOMINOES Your Choice

Read *Dominoes* for pleasure, or to develop language skills. It's your choice.

Each *Domino* reader includes:

- a good story to enjoy
- integrated activities to develop reading skills and increase vocabulary
- task-based projects – perfect for CEFR portfolios
- contextualized grammar activities

Each *Domino* pack contains a reader, and an excitingly dramatized audio recording of the story

If you liked this *Domino*, read these:

Lord Arthur Savile's Crime and Other Stories

Oscar Wilde

The three stories in this book are about ordinary people, people like you and me; but they find themselves in surprising situations. Lord Arthur Savile, a rich man with no enemies, finds out that he must do something terrible before he can marry. Poor young Hughie Erskine gives money to an old beggar – but the beggar is not what he seems. And Lord Murchison falls in love with a mystery woman – but what is the strange secret behind the door in Cumnor Street?

The Drive to Dubai

Julie Till

When his father is arrested in Dubai, Kareem has to move fast. He must show that his father is not a thief – and prove that his family is honest. For Kareem is going to marry the beautiful and intelligent Samira Al-Hussein, and she could never marry someone from a bad family.

So Kareem and his brother get to work quickly – with a little help from Samira.

	CEFR	Cambridge Exams	IELTS	TOEFL iBT	TOEIC
Level 3	B1	PET	4.0	57-86	550
Level 2	A2–B1	KET-PET	3.0-4.0	–	390
Level 1	A1–A2	YLE Flyers/KET	3.0	–	225
Starter & Quick Starter	A1	YLE Movers	1.0–2.0	–	–

You can find details and a full list of books and teachers' resources on our website: www.oup.com/elt/gradedreaders